Common Sense

WESLEYAN POETRY

Common Sense

Ted Greenwald

WESLEYAN UNIVERSITY PRESS
Middletown, Connecticut

Wesleyan University Press
Middletown CT 06459
www.wesleyan.edu/wespress
© 1978 Ted Greenwald
All rights reserved
Manufactured in the United States of America

First Wesleyan University Press edition 2016
Originally published in 1978 by L Publications

Some of these poems appeared in the following magazines: *Adventures in Poetry, Angel Hair, Another World* (Bobbs-Merrill), *Big Sky, Blue Pig, The Human Handkerchief, Lapstrake* (Lines Books), *The Life* (Big Sky Books), *Lines, Making a Living* (Adventures in Poetry), *Miami* (Doones Press), *The Midatlantic Review, Native Land* (Titanic Books), *The New Money* (*Blue Pig* #19, Sand Project Press), *New York Times, Ocultist Witness, Paris Review, Park Row, Roof, Shirt* (Doones Press), *Short Sleeves* (Buffalo Press), *Sun, This, WB, The World.*

Library of Congress Control Number: 2015956640

Paperback ISBN: 978-0-8195-7642-2
Ebook ISBN: 978-0-8195-7643-9

5 4 3 2 1

to WIG and SEG

CONTENTS

Common Sense

WHIFF

An evening
Spent talking
Spent thinking
About what my life would be
If I'd stayed
With a particular girl or woman
I went with
What would be
If I'd've been accepted to and gone
Where I applied
To a different school
Than the one I did
Where I'd learned
Different social graces
Than the ones I have
Where some of the material
Values of the American dream
Had rubbed off
Enough to make me
Live it out
In the good-works sense
If I'd settled down
And settled
For the foundation
On a house
For future generations
Instead of assuming
Immediately past generations
My foundation to mine
If I'd been
A little quicker to learn
What was expected of me

And wanting to please pleased
Going on that way
Through all eternity
I've probably been saved
From mere routines
By a streak of stubbornness
By a slow mind
And tendency to drift
By an emotional development
That requires
My personal understanding
Before happening
Feeling out the implications
An emotion has in
Form of expectation
Before trying out and
After awareness
I sense a willingness
To tell someone
I know and like
And sense the same from
Anything they'd like to know
About me
And, at the same time, have
A vast sense of privacy
Which means
There's no way
I'll wear out my personality
And its sense of continuity
Although sometimes
I feel empty
But talking to
Someone I like
And trust

And sense the same from
I feel way up
And after a long evening
Of talk about this and that
Feel wide awake
And feel the world
Wide and awake around me
And have a visual intensity
In memory
That, in near memory, dulls
And throbs
And grows vivid as hell
When I bring it to mind
Some time from then
What my life
Would've been like
Under different circumstances
Would've been different
With its own
Attendant ifs
And its own what-might've-been
But this way
I've elected to follow
And cast my vote
Each waking day in
I avoid
The possibility
Of taking the past too seriously
Or feeling any bitterness
Or sadness
This way
When my ship comes in
I'll've passed out of mind
Beyond the sight of land

And won't hesitate
For a second
To look back on all this
With fondness or remiss
The air'll be clear
The moon'll be there
And you, whoever
You are and hope to be,
Will be here with my love

FOG ROLLED IN

fog rolled in
drink rolled down
water towers
cars sixteen floors down (night)
wind in, cool off the room
seen *The Quiet Man* (homeric)
my brain feels homeric in its dawning
Joan up in Ithaca (my arms cool)
reading at Holly's a week from tonight
readings reel in my brain
plans reel in my brains
to marry Joan (secretly of course)
to set up *our* house (better wishes bad feelings
cautions lay to rest) a place to live for two people
life a subtheme
drink cooling my throat, a new notebook underway
the night in place
the night in a place in my heart in my doubts
my fingers itch (for what)   I
loosen them, the self
rests in the night   it is asleep now   this poem
is awake   underneath the poem is a dream   soon
the dream will be all over

P.S.

Enormously difficult
To explain *exactly*
How I feel
Clearing my brain
After seeing
Where I'm going
After resting
After taking care of this and that
For another round of works
Finished one thing
Found a *solid* voice
(Temporary, I'm sure)
Time to lean back
And think about life
Roughly halfway over
(Over what?   Water?)
Very little
In the way of theory
Cropping up (like grass)
More and more
The time turns to practice
The sense of unity
I feel should be somewhere
I guess'll be there
Long after I'm gone
And someone else
Looks back on all this
And talks to me
Across the ages
With me talking
Through my poems
Up to a certain point

(A hundred, two hundred years)
Language (the ass) carries
The burden of meaning
While after (say
Around five hundred years hence)
A flipflop (oops, a pothole!)
The meaning carries
The language
By then (like me)
Changed beyond recognition
And to think
This doesn't even require
A grand plan
Although, if I recall correctly,
At one time
I thought it did
And had one
Ready for anything
Nowadays I'm more or less content
To let a lot
Of things take their own courses
Like amiable rivers
Making blue lines
Down the map of history
I'm not saying
That some things
Don't infuriate me
They certainly do
But I've learned
Mostly through stupid repetition
The same patience
I apply to my own works
Moving them out of range of good and evil
Is applicable

(In a romantic way, I guess)
To things (natural and unnatural)
Outside myself
I'm on better terms
(Though still able to bear grudges)
With most things and people
More sociably amiable
(No longer stand
In a corner at parties
Facing into the wall
Smelling the school-like plaster
Getting plastered)
Now I talk it up
And even when down
Never talk down
But remain subdued
I've learned to like
Winters more
But hate the end of same
Feel relief at spring
Crave sun on body
Enter through the lobby
Of annual depression
Have greater sense of
Personal comfort
Expanding horizons
Ability to survive
(And know how far I'll go
To do)
In this year of famine
And pestilence
Have learned
To keep my mind and ear
Cocked (like a gun)

For the true poetry
Of the language to go off
And fill
The sky of the mind
With angels conversing
And have
Enough memory left
To remember
And write the angels down
Without pinning
A single body or wing
I have finally
Returned to the cheerfulness
I had when very young
Before the bubbles
In my personal seltzer'd
Gone flat
When the fingers of school
Having opened my thinking cap
Kept the bottle open
Long enough
To let the fun out
Amidst a multitude of others
Asking one way or another
"Whatever happened to you?
You were such a cheerful kid"
And that I am

AIRY RUSHES PUNCH

Airy rushes punch my shirt
Through a window of sunset dirt
And send me reeling like a lure
Through the water nerves of America
Once on the other side of somewhere
I relax and become someone else
Not that I behave different
Just behave less often
The sky offers me solace and office space
And stars I keep in drawers
Wear nothing
But a little mist and halo
I will imagine myself
A sympathetic headlight
Knocking on the door of the night
To borrow a cup of sugar
From the beautiful neighbor
Who's moved in
Without even the clothes on her back
"Would it be possible
To borrow a cup of sugar"
"Sure   Sit down, honey
Make yourself comfortable"
I ease down in the big dipper

BLEEP

Somewhere (where) in between say
Index and middle fingers, to one day
Wake up and find growing a new rather
Radish vestigial finger
Little do you know little do you too know
Questions.   Eyes picking off barrages of mirages soberly.
Lone. Drinking on an empty beach. Sauterne
Bottle overturned. Sand thru sievey fingers,
Listen to prokprok of waves
Fearing too many great many great
Thinkers and thinkers of our time
Busy themselves, usefully. Seeing sprockets as the real
Real.   (And all *that* entails.
Spend time dubbing in historical consciousness,
Makes the heart grow blonder with the distance.
Waterproofs hair. Air.
Fingernails grow whatever way you wish
Sunny nostalgia the way wishes grow,
Whicheverway, are more close to
OBJECTIVE vestments searched for where
Disguised as rockets
One's free to choose between limits
Between sign that YIELD
Either a b c d e or
Any other squint or
Sequence found squeezing the fingers.   Eh, graft.   Being
Not so much a question of question or of answer,
Swallowed with unicap and orange juice, but of right
Detachment from the lips
Alphabetically precipitate, that really brings out
Evening crickets bats the real you eating bubbles
Every and each night of the week, depends

Combining sequence with each (vague) COUNT.

Always hoped for sixth toe on either foot.

Merely sonar, an indication you're not alone

And someone somewhere cares for you.

Detailly, even if vaguely.   Please, to mow the maudlin.

FOR TED, ON ELECTION DAY

for Ted Berrigan

rain (second day in a row)
morning (day-after-day)
body smell, need a bath
coffee cigarets ashes in ashtrays
one-after-another pile up
need shoes, yesterday walking
in rain revealed a hole in my right sole
sitting around not thinking of much of anything
feeling drizzly, wait to go vote (later)
'no' to mass transit amendment
have my fill of mass transport
everyone wanting to transport themselves
went to Columbia (last night) to hear
Ron read translations (one of four readers, translators)
fine translations drinking opium
through pores of ordinary american
unlike the others (studies in the subordinate clause)
(non) relation to (any) poetry
first school setting for me in 4 years (puke!)
vergule
everything starting to fit in place
have a home
be a home   home
reaping (this fall) routines
reappearing in the dress of melancholy like
the housewife of a house
making (work) time go
I've made some money working with my own hands
I've made some working with my own hands
I've made up much
experienced some done some

I've loved often enough

been shot down enough to hurt often

I've pitied myself as well as others (both ways unhealthy emotion)

I've wondered if I *could* love someone else (morbid)

I've made my doubts into poems

discovering covers often get kicked off

to cool the body's heat and mind's jungle growth

I've wondered (and felt made to wonder) if my own 'worth' is

'worth much' and wavered

well, Ted, when I saw you on 8th St last month

we (you) talked for awhile and

then went over St. Mark's and Gem's to take pictures with Gerard

you said, the one thing that always disturbed you

about my poems

is there are no *really* embarrassing moments

in them (I couldn't get a word in edgewise, you were holding forth)

I don't really know what's embarrassing, shot elastic in panties

              at a party that drop and stop conversations

              turn heads?

who knows   ('who knows' embarrasses me)

and anyway there's quite a difference between gossip and

   embarrassment

(couldn't get a word in edgewise, for two hours)

what embarrasses me is

I'm 28 and aware (and made aware) of it all the time

I'm finding it difficult to stop smoking (still 3 pks a day)

and have been drinking too much lately (out of what, boredom

              habit, pain?   don't know, who knows)

smoking too much dope

irritates the shit out of my nervous system

being continuously irritated (snapping)

putting on weight

plagued by small aches and pains (right now open abscess draining

              behind my right ball, can't sit)

think I have trouble sleeping (and, I guess, really don't)
my habits and routines embarrass me
and I still, although I don't think so as much, think my arms
                              too skinny (they *really* aren't)
my body too small or too big (varies from day-to-day)
it's embarrassing to feel
my self body image etc (often)
defined by people around me (my reaction to their reactions)
that embarrasses me a lot
zeal embarrasses me, your zeal for instance
always lining up poets and their poems
one up one down
in relation to you and your poems
(I'm embarrassed by the same zeal, ambitions,
it's no real consolation that when it rains it rains on everyone)
most of all, this Election Day, I'm embarrassed by death
death is really the only embarrassing thing
and sometimes (unexpectedly these days more often)
it scares the shit out of me

AND, HINGES

Fog hanged over the park, the night cold, and, clean
against the tree you leaned in the sunlight, breathing
he spinned the car out on fine gravel near the gate
she laughing at the tree   standing straggly   over the fence.

And, the drain clogs, when I shower, with my hair,
queasily, paper rolling out of your handbag, glinting sequins,
and, she stood, laughing   over her shoulder   by the spinning
  wheels
"how do you get to the station, from here?"

Skin   smelling clean, after the shower, and, dark,
merrily, tempting   me to talk to you, and, asking if you've seen,
and, turning to her friend, tall, and, skinny next to her,
"Taking the first   turning you come to   in the book, and curve

round it."   Warm moisture rising, I rise sluggishly,
the latest news from Paris, tho I've never been there, calm
"he never could control the damn thing, and, thinks he's Fangio."
She knew better than to laugh, but she did   anyway   , laughing

hide behind a tree, and, light bark late, keeping the neighbors late,
and, you ask me "have you seen the latest news from Paris?"
Out back someone   mugging laughter   , and, he thought over the
  problem
to bust her gut.   "Did you see that turning   the horse   made
  dog?"

Hours arranged handily on the wrist, I scrutinize them,
and, and tell you "I've never been there myself, have you?"
How to get back on the road, and, keeping his hands intact.
"Absolutely splendor, the light on   shimmering her hand."

Hourly, and, after dinner they scrutinize me.   "How we love,"
and, you answer, "yes, dozens of times."   I look at my watch
He's such a bore.   Always running around fast over the place."
She knew better than to know   know better than his local hands,
    placed

filling mail order slips, out, sleeping afterward   in the down,
and, you shiver, and, laugh, "it's really terrible what's happening!"
how it sounds in reverse.   Scared, and, the hairs turning prematurely
gray, respectably, over the nearest sand mound in the pile

pillow I puff up with my hand   before the light   goes out
"oh yes, I agree, would you care to join me for lunch,"
spun gravel rising under the wheels, and, him sitting.   The clay
    lump
she picked up some too, running it thru   her veiled fingers

in the fireplace.   And, you say "you are thirsty," and, I believe,
and, you take my hand, handily switching your pursing lips
to the other side clinging higher under the screech, and, wheel.
And, she looked at him, blinking owlly back tears.   And, they

came anyway, you, and, "I am thirsty too, for more dinner wine"
"not having any money, but wanting to speak to you so much."
"Who?   Who?   Does he think he is?   Anyway?"
She knew there was nothing to do but curve out the light ground

under her, and, several more candles to warm the room.   To the other
side of your mouth.   "That's okay, I love lunch in the park, anyhow."
His phantom figure stalking shadow after shadow after dark.
And, cry til a little pool formed, and, she rose to go home.

STOP FOR

stop for
a minute
wait up
for this
friend to
tick off
its catching
breath and
draw parallel
like two
lines with
two el's
the train
of thought
reaches the
station in
the Bronx
or Queens
the friends
get off
at and
walk out
of below
onto the
french tablecloth
of sun
in a
black and
white movie
in one
of those
theaters with
a sky

NOTE TO A DUMB FRIEND

how long's it been
since we last spoke
there are infinitely less
bridges left
than last a lifetime
weather's finally gotten nice
the sky in t-shirt
how's yourself   the kids
must be grown a lot
since I last saw them
has the job been working
out all right   everything
's pretty much the same
here, but a little better,
if *that* makes any sense
the sun's on the scene
the tiniest random bolt
blocks away glows
despite rust   windows
and brick take on a fire
you wouldn't expect
this I'd miss if I was
n't here   that, and
dinner with friends
you haven't been down
to see the apartment yet
—the one I share— so I
can only approximate the view
the rent is nothing in
comparison   the state of
the nation, body politic
corrupt body that houses

the dog's skeleton is
nothing   even the glowing
nerve-ends of buildings
are nothing to the vertical
pleasure harvested from
the horizontal   don't
get me wrong   my feet
are still very much on
the ground   my feet are
grounded in sacred principles
that carry me to sharpen
my wits on the whetstone
of today's air   suddenly
we've passed all that
on a train of thought with
a hook in it to reach out
and grasp the male principle
in the station just passed
this allows us to nap in
comfort for awhile, letting,
like efficiently circulating
blood, the breeze gently
blow around the toe
managing to *move* me a foot
from where I started
but, enough about me
how about you

THE/SKELETON

the
skeleton
of
the
gestures
were
glowing

PORE SUSPENSION

I'm having a hard time making ends meet
So what, my suit is tan, that is the style
What with the grocery bills being
What they are. Do you have the same trouble
Now. And you know damn well that that is the way
Adding 2 and 2 and getting uneasy,
Strange numbers you never thought existed before?
I like it: when the style changes so does my tie;
It is not really the strangeness you are
Talking about. It might be the coloring,
You can hear me huffing (puff) (puff)
But never the strangeness. That is beastly.
Or, at least hot. The numbers creeping up
Going down the street away from your door
Behind you in your head, as you sit smoking
The ash growing longer with the hours.
After you have had the last word in the conver-
It is the longest cigaret
You ever smoked.
Sensationally, speaking of our love, it is on the fritz,
Part of the new german-french lover from "New Vague"
Invading the number system

PRIVETS COME INTO SEASON AT HIGH TIDE

Privets come into season at high tide.
The night on the Great Neck side
near Steppingstone the bargeman walks
over the water the refrigerator opened the mailman fell out.
Opening the closet the grocery boy fell out
banging his head on the floor his knee.
The snow bushes 40 years preparing dinner,
or the laugh on the rug, gold threads weaving in
& out over the bodies on the floor.
First sack, the corrugated box lit up
under the lawn lamp the rippled footsteps
running from the scene of the hiding, tumbled out on-
to the floor. "What are you doing in there?"
"I am searching. It is good to be free again."

The first race we took a beating
lurching free from the vain control of sense.
As your hair goes so
goes the subtle undercurrents passing thru the foot in-
to the chin, & up. Even if you ground
yourself with the closet door the tension
is mixed, the filth of corners have no effect
& proselytic airs the room have no effect.
The hum. The prop limbs stacked in the corner
penetrate handle & space between finger-
tip plastered the original conviction.

Dialogue:
white hair melting in the warm air
rising from the radiator in the corner, the whiteness.
The hand. The space between fingers.
Walking slowly on the rocks.

Character:
nubile
syrup the syrup
marrow from the lips of well
the spray, the seaweed, her grass side,
sweating with a light touch on the neck,
walking the ghastly hours deliveries are made;
dotted hours, & the rabid denture chewing the long gloss.

Her maple thigh—mole . . . cheek —
the chattering of teeth on the ground,
count out plums & grapes
leading the eyelid bay & stars.   The line.
The whim drawing the danger thru the dust out of the corner.
The underbrush kelp.   Transforming the hedge circuits.

THE / FORM

the
form
of
the
words
pump
blood
in
the
form
of
the
heart

MIAMI

for Ed. Baynard

buildings blend
into the sky   the work
goes on
from where we left off
and consciousness, by rights,
is doors and windows
a spritz of color
in this life
is what we can expect
if we can expect anything
and a breeze or two
a quiet day   a little sun
that 5-letter word "money"
relying on no one
for pleasure
than the weather and the then
discovered leisure
to lean a little
into more than can be expected
let me explain
we feel the heart
against the ribs
we feel the leg
against the chair
we feel two eyes linked as one
looking into your two
and rubbing your brow
like a finger
taking the sweat lengthwise
off the brow and drying the forehead
which is suddenly your

we feel the nouns make emotions
out of a sense of easiness
the ability to relax
the desire to simplify
what we suddenly discover
is meant
because we haven't paid attention
to exemplify something
what it is, we forget
we know it was something special
something out of the ordinary
a nagging something or other
stupidly repeating itself
in a vague way
on the sill
when we think the water still
that's the silliest thing
I ever heard of
hearing everything through
the air conditioner above
the bottom line

QUICK

coffee
farm
desire for quiet
desire for dream
arabesque farm
the imagination curves
goes on for a long while
walks
rests
comes to a halt
rests
curves again
spot a little town
curves again, this time back
reverse comma
coffee (throat curves)
neck farm
hills roll
moves on
goes for some distance
doglegs to the right
goes north to alaska
curves
follows the humboldt current
rewinds
takes off is airborne
grows silver wings
burrows deeply
a stranger walks in and out
expands
an eyelash
semi-colon

eyebrow   :
the farm waits
coffee return
curves
curves
while waiting for a bus
kept in check
sled
leading man
tick along
a film suddenly grows
a bubble
a bubble suddenly grows a butterfly
wings curve
a butterfly suddenly grows
a winged forehead
curve around a thought farm
desire curves
desire misses a curve and wakes up
far field

HIS / (THE

his
(the
poet's
lines
often
reflect
(like
an
echo)
a
concern
with
mortality
and
life
(his
and
the
world's
her's)

DETONATOR

Carbines crowd memory
if you think that way
Bernouli did   Each night
brooding over a glass of milk
lines of flow around airfoil
fondles an old moroccan moon
discovering
while weighing niceties of weather and air,
wind direction, flipflop of earth,
and other sundries
lines of flow around airfoil
yank at the yangtse
A)   corresponds to a plane in level flight
Above wing a region of increased velocity and reduced
pressure arcs of love sent as a souvenir of Mi
ami a bag of pecans "wishing you were here"
below wing pressure nearly atmospheric
"Vanilla custard face melting"
tanned and blonding
to volunteer trying a return sortee
"Into your lap"
parks and gardens meet heartway
between lions in front of the NYPL
and looks, like dandelions
and dandelionly impress heads together
into a petalled telephone directory of Weehawken
that glances off the top part of a cloud
sets up a region of whirls and eddies
leads to complications
palming off fingers fingernails
"following an altogether impersonal whim"

You detan on the trip north
and feel
depressed altho you to this isnt apparent, but is
"your profile"
at the first glance of you in months
thru coved glass at the airport
rises in sun and reflects a wire
statue tingles bronze in fountain center
behind schedule
fluorescent bouillon of compressed paper
birches ceiling with light whiffs
transparent nude
tint over pennies on bottom of the pool,
eyes lapse lap
Stall
Taking edge off
what languor this inner cylinder, O,
gull tassels shoot from behind clouds
and brings on damps
of overexercise of the mind
that quite levels a lasso of stars
surreptitiously combined to constellate
what new fought for new piques
assail you from behind a wing
as achronic charley horse

                    A hem
It isnt really a quince shun or guava
white to pink
of over and under   Its not even
a repository for sealing wax and the secret ring
you seal your letters with
with a wink
altho theyre extruded under your aruba nails

harden to a bright puce
It's not really anything anyway that has to do
halfmoon to full
with you
or with a laser state that appears
in light of the pings
starting out as nothing but a bad case
all allure
of the heebyjeebies
leading to an overindulgence
in inessential terminals
No matter what you think of it it has nothing to do
with a force that tends
to drag liquid into an interior cylinder
which instantly takes abcd shape
brings pangs for laminar of past
occuring during complete consciousness
in a balloon floating over rockies
various mountain changes
cuts loose from the very thinnest of pressurized veils
pours essays leisurely over a catalogue of new haunts
appears to the visual imagination

in a thighlength skirt
as water
and causes a drop of mysterious fluid in milk
to dissolve precipitously
after warning by crinkles was received hundreds of times
warned about saturation point
consequence of motion
coming to you out of sequence via satellite
disguised as a pat of butter
you watch melt in a soggy baked potato
with a garden of cream and chives in it held together by rubberbands

Strange selves of shelves making up cliffhangers
Those convex links
to be watched carefully so you can see sun
reflected from them
as a selfhelp portions of light
arches and aches melting from a millimeter of stucco
losing train of transverse dimension
that is so close that
is so close as to be without pinpoints
ready to fire away at perspiration lesions
disguised as lemon drops
breathlessly crushing the skull   :
"creatures are said to die of consumption,"
and,
grass between web blades   Dew blaze

RADIO CROP

radio crop

train at home in your spare time

homebodies

a cloud on
a stamp on
a postcard in
a mailbox, wing
to you (to you)

love repeats itself in repairs

you repair to
the slot where
the card from me
fell to you (to you)

love, from me

DEW, DISCREPANCY

And in retrospect I'll
cease pacing   Mint
jalousies in the porch door   Aluminum
frame   Might as well be a harp
Harpstring   Thru open
slats, west wind   Buzz,
slats   Glass tune
Rayly lats flex
Hands fingers nails quiver
Generator worms into the ear
What runt's this delights stirs Isis
What, what   Song
wherein
the cricket swallows
its own heart   What
And let me say
vermiculate cheeks, tear motor
Earlier, riffling thru the codex
(Thorax?
moon cinderblock gray trapped
in a bath for good thru a ripple,
seeks a sunnier page, sun glyph
floats retrospectively, I
find a gusty solstice
standing adroitly over water
find $8^1/_2 \times 11$ adorable
packaged twined indicative of
my own lie   shadow undereye   What lie
Of two legs, rippling intersection   What
my body carmine line   A liar
where its own self's concerned
Tern (elf) prints peer in sand,

where   Ignorance of
dirt under the nails   Let's say, ignoring
an intersection, praying to listen to
a spider walk on water   Pray   Pray   Ha
Greenly proceeding the eyes
Warp internecine tears
Watch, expressly jealous
moving over the surface
that's soundless, that   whey habit
surfeits fat pockets of the face
Pond skimmer's ripple emanate
from four pods
seminating apatetic
qua belladonna
(wine and cure
caloric throwaway, away
what lies otherwise
camouflage as noise as poise
of white sheet on a line,
dry wind on the line
or heart failure
(bass eye
put it on the line

A THOUGHT

a thought
brings back a memory
of a dream
in a lobby
of a hotel
with a train in the station
                a plane
describes what I see
through the motor of wire
completing the diagram of desire
with a flower finish
my eyes
follow each petal
and detach the finish
from the stem of the verb
while the brain
detaches from the brain-stem
which I didn't mind
this is life
not like in the movies

I HEAR A STEP

1

I hear a step. A step.
The piping on the side of the couch
patterns of roses & the wispy stem of
rolled cloth dangling from the lip.
The first time it was hard coping with your breasts
magnolias cutting patterns from the clouds.
My feet crunch pinecones.
You were beneath me on the couch, the cushion,
the floor. I don't remember. Still.
You flung sounds at me. The silence.

Snow covered the ground between the barn & farmhouse.
A fleck of snow buried itself in the rooster's skull.
The skin was cold. The heat off for the evening.
You draped your mouth with feathers & flowers.
The muffled kiss.
Snow on your neck, the collar of your coat grazing your cheeks.
I am used to the grain now. It tastes circuitous.

2   CAPSULE

I swallowed early this morning the highway burning my foot.
The gingerbread on the edge of the roof.
Twin peaks rise to the lightning, explode,
a web of vine leaves exhausting the vane's tip
sink in a swell of dust. Still.

The distance between your fingers, & the water when you swallow,
bloats my eyes — waiting for the puffing of rug,
piled muffins, one-by-one in your mouth —

the campfire relieving the shadow of the dawn on the road.
A sleepy fox crosses the zig-zag of the road resting
between segments.   I am hungry
& eat leaves along the edge of the straight shoulder.

3   BREAKOUT

The distance.   A black car pulls to the side of the road.
The Cow got out piling the raincoat collar at the neck.
"Will he be ready?   We have a long trip ahead."

The narrow granite wall explodes clearing the smoke.
He steps out onto your foot the floor of the road the sinking gravel.

"Ready?"   He nodded.   The distance disappeared in
the car moving down the road tiptoeing round the curve.

FAT LINES, TURN

fat lines, turn
through the first turn
the car makes turning
along the highway   ending
the turn a solid white
line says "don't turn
yet, wait till you check
rearview mirror for oncoming
traffic, pick up speed, then turn"
maybe a second elapses
when the turn is compiled
and you are speeding north
you notice signs of
everything turning to spring

TRACER

how can
I get at
this flypaper
sticking
in my head
next to the smell
of wet grape
and a small
grapeless
skin of wine
how can
I get at
this tile
crumbling
in my head
next to the taste
of a wet grape
and small grapeless
skin of wine
how can
I get at
this skin
crumbling
in my head
next to taste
of a wet grape
and a small
grapeless
skin of wine
how can
I get out
this touch of wet skin

crushed
in my head
next to the taste
of a wet grape
and a small
grape
skin of wine

FOUR DAYS OF BOOKS AND HIGH FEVER

four days of books and high fever
descends its ecstasy over my throat
weighted the whole time like a pannier
graced with notes like a piano
emptying keys in the
drawer of my ear
a passion lets loose its paints
pressing wildly the buttons to tubes to the
hair I've lost patience with put on end
told to stay there   the hair ignores
and slams doors in my face easing out
the elevator across the lobby in a wave

I FORGOT TO REMEMBER

I forgot to remember
whether I was supposed
to take you to the moon
and put you in the palm
and take you home again
does this ring a bell (a bell)
did you remember
how dusty the cheese did taste
did you bring any cigarets
long after we're dust
do you think we'll trust
ourselves to wipe clean
the wiped table
did you bring anything
for me to eat
can you wing everything
from memory
what am I doing here
talking to myself in martian
when I could be
on the beach taking in the ocean
lean this way like a breeze
O, wonderful breeze
and whisper
what you know in my ear
I hope I please you
I hope to squeeze you
like an orange
disk with both our names
on it climbing
like monkeys
to the top of the chart

I forgot to mention
I remembered our heart

TRANSFORMATIONAL GRAMMAR

diverse living languages
slot hotels
performing 'native words'
brief comment
rose rituals flaunt hot
group 'dialects'
africa america 'name'
the 'part(s) of speech'
tickle phonetic alphabets
smooth as possible
the more common grammar
stress the verb *to be*
be terrific be great be
quick cool be been

LAPSTRAKE

The cleat curved you curved the spider
the coil of alcoholic fumes
the webbing of sail & sunset,
over the mountain the distance : Colorado,
New Mexico.   In Tucson
the beggars are gymnasts good riders swaying side-to-side
are fine steerers covering much territory
the backroom towel & soap the front leg.

The drainpipe of your leg the lapstrake side of the shipping
the barge traveling at speeds incredible to the eyes
in the movement of lips carpeting seaweed with
pitch & roll of the movements of your leg,
your lips the errors of your back lingered on your chest
when the spider came to milk the thread of your leg
the bending the back or arch
the cleat punctuating gulls, or blue packet.

Stemming the flow of guitar music
craving the movement of the arm, the total movement,
from the sleep tarantulaic
iodine in the mouth
the leg moving over the hills
the horses frothing at the inn black hairs draping
your breasts with prairie roses, the rope on
the side of the saddle the movement of the cleat tying up the ship
side lapstraking the breeze
Juno nibbling at 20th century foliage, the seaweed,
iodine the mouth watering at the sight of the spider,

the hovering movement of the facets
leggings moving up the thighs in a crawl

up the mountains the search for the rope hanging at the saddle
the mounting of the easy charge thru the streets
Cheyenne, Yuma in the afternoon the border the night before
nibbling at the conscientious boundary.
"make good time?"
"more than thrifty miles or the devil's league.   the cactus is boring."
"are you carrying spare parts of hair?   leg?   or other?"
only several drinks to unparch the deck
the reeking odor of major feet in the mountain,
slicking down package of roots to chase
in the distance lying under a scrub the gray remnants of rug
the gray pellets of shoes & legs
bathing the horses in the pool.

He would never make the border & the meat tasted
fine the fire burning his tongue, trying to relieve
the tension of the first mask, the second
wave of iodine cluttering his tongue,
the web the tastiness of tongue on flesh.

COMMON SENSE

a
sense
of
balance
takes
a
sense
of
balance

SOMETHING NICE HAPPENED

something nice happened
today   I got a call
from someone who
told me someone else
who we both know well
who I don't see
much anymore because
the mutual someone
drinks too much and
's a foul drunk
got hepatitis   and is okay
now but can't drink
for a year   and I think
this is nice   this is *terrific*
this makes the new year
one to look forward to, maybe

ONE / THING

one
thing
I'm
sure
of
is
launched

WE PASS SLOWLY

we pass slowly
in the fingers of light
composing, in shadow, a
hand on the glass building
we part at the corner
like hair and wave
bye   we mix deeply
within sweet waters
where memory turns
green with envy, spits
out sky-blue   the small
of the back of afternoon
passes   we each turn
and watch the hand
fit smoothly over the ass
and feel the body
melt over the mind

JIGGLES

targets cluster . (or is it) targets huddle .
(my) headache's been with me for 3 days .
unsettling (my) eyes settle in a cloud .

(or is it) (my) ,
eyes settle on a cloud .
or my (is it)
eyes settle
or on (is it)
my , eyes settle in (is it) a cloud
on or in
a settle
(my) cloud (or is it)

mud (my) (or it) is
whatever (my) eyes
make of
(on) or (in)
the settling
(or) the cloud , it
is (my) (or)
is (or) it
my cloud

hugging the tugs . (is it) (my) tuggings hug .
on- (or) in-
to (is it) days settle in a headache .

ELEGANCE AND UMBRELLAS

To assume a new character, when the old one wore
Near me, so "lonely" when night   to darken
Paired with polar stars sinking over Paris
Moves in   over the dusty coast
And dreamed up a girl "deja vue"
Out. In years days say hours,
The room, the road broad leaves shivering   in the wind
Moves slowly over the Atlantic toward New York.
Shuffling thru an old picture   of you.
I'm all mixed up about things
Your bone structure's receding   in gell
Her hair free   in a winding cone
I snoozed right under a palm tree, cocoanut oil
A *vade mecum* of equi   vocal means and ways   to
Go to seed imaginatively, and besides I'm lonely without you
Behind my eyes a rising
Bowl of gold dust making the sea oily.
Due west from Paris   a mote of a girl
"Deja"
Say seconds : all things beginning to wear
Expanding out glossside to dull   with each gust
Dovetailing a neaping tide of glaciers
Coastly larved in her eyes. Remember in her eyes
Purring neutrally
Swaying in in my rumor
Leaning into a new skin
Of your old hairs musting in the corner.
Locale floating outside,
That too is fading blue swirl
Purring for a way out   from behind a mobile wall
Or a new set of bumps reveling character on my skull,
Shuffles thru "an old picture

Of you"   in reverse   crust
Tincolor, in eye corners, gray eyes,
Give away the recipe for new character
You brush away with a back of the hand :
Is the percolator off?
Why do your ears glow :
So :
In a plastic jar,
Elastic yeast, orbit of the adrenalin fanatic.
Belonging there, that was all, a part
The degree of change possible
On either side of the Atlantic
Palm out, flapping leaves over with hurricane strength
At midnight   under lid climatic conditions
The odor of drying mud on the upper lip
"A mote of a girl" :
Con
Templating dinky boats tossed like marble breads :
In the wind rising from the northeast.
"Lonely"   then trees rising fur to the wind
Silver as neck and spine mustang ease pose
That leaves "alone" landscape combed
Clouds maple from three points   from a thumb
Smoothing back my cowlick
For itself, in bump form. Salad
Mold darkens in my "dusty" palms
Or, lacuna loafs "lonely"
Between the gold stretching coast-to-coast
New York to Paris   "with dullside out"
Where I was stranded.   Grain shade in New York
Rays of sun point setting the way   over the hills
Molding in a jello map
From prominent bumps   of landscape or seascape
Whatever time it is   I'm lonely without you

Remember you from copper outlining pleated with disappearing spaces
Getting the feel "of the landscape" and making predictions.
If I take everything weighed from the coast
Until only posse space was left, working into me
For the future , from multiplying bumps   on the beach
"I'm still lonely without you"
Away from the center   mortising canticles   remains dead
Cursing the bump I was worn under, like under a star
Behind her eyes in back of your ming,
Thunderheads hammock wriggle to hum eraser pink, in sum,
Objections dart,
Drying up,   fur blowing over the sea
Due west from Paris covered with elegance and umbrellas.

COMB

clean glass
brushable
a shock
something familiar insignia
fingers gold control
better still
open-ended capped
delicate pressure
nature steps present
mental image of color
a drink
a swim
a face
body forth
can be or has been
hesitation
lean, waltz

FATTY

modules of work

> the window
> the nearest exit
> the first year
> the rehearsal

comes into the foreground

> a pass
> a space
> a bell rings
> a window
> a stunt

goes out of the picture

> break up
> mobilize
> profile
> tension
> open

delay trifles in slow motion

> q. his scramble
> c. common sense
> v. in one hall
> t. beforehand

breaks the inertia of the logical

hands a key to the first passer-by

grow bigger as they go away

imagine on paper what he sees and feels

natural

a motive

an office in the eye

MAKING A LIVING

its method
is men
the fact
and the game
disorder
grounded
expressed
real named
the facts of life
the planet
its field

the same day
vehicles
lived by the masses
become
contemplative
attitudes
powered by
the joys of this world
a glorious sign
propagated with
lightning speed

at the same time
its goal
the use of time
the speed of transport
the margin of life
the rational
journeys
by another path
none of it bad

the work
from his world
themselves
rediscovers nature
its essential green
easily seen through
like a window
but intimate
like a summer meadow

as a result
cold dreams
draw misty truths
to the surface
official forgetfulness
looks back on
and chooses
to forget
the first half of
to focus discussion on
the second half
like "I'm fine"
as a journey
all to itself
and beautiful
to the voyager
particularly

this service
its servants
our passage of time
vanishes quickly
like a leaf
its eulogy

a terrestrial paradise
the very spirit of
the renaissance
to act
on the basis of

an obsession with death

well,
death

pronounce it
be-u-ti-full
slowly revealed
to eliminate
this lived time
men live in
sea turtles
to the laws

ZERO HOUR

the
shepherd
's function
was to play
the flute
dance
country dances
and serve
fruit and wine
daintily
to his rulers
to act
(in other words)
as beauty to
beautiful people

A MAN WAS ON A HILL

a man was on a hill
looking down in the valley
of interest when he noticed
something funny going on
he put his glasses to his eyes
and said "something
funny's going on, what could
it be, where is it, there it is"
summer changed to fall
and the man kept his eyes
glued to the speck that was
always before him
winter changed to spring and
still the speck didn't budge
the man said said to himself "some-
thing funny's going on
and I'm going to find out
what it is"   a pleasurable
room struck his brain

MISTER TREE'S MANUAL

I'm in the flower pot here
I turn my head away from the sun
When rain falls, I'm my happiest
If you listen closely as I do to grass grow

I could think of no better way to
I move to infinitive
As the airline I wag does too
Drawing closer and closer to a perfect score

I shift with each drawn shade
I room with the room
As well as gathering dust, I bathe daily
Perking when sun goes down

I change colors in midafternoon
I break up the floor in cube squares
Rooming in the room, I jump up and down
Laffing sideways between limes

I hinge colors in a drawl
I dry myself with each vowel
Sneak up behind each consonant, I tsk
Riding off with the room into the sunset

I change horses
I remember to inspect the road
Altho cooling thru the day, I wake up
And go to sleep with no so so dream lace

I guess I could go on forever
I could

Dying to meet you, I lean toward fire
Caressing newspaper puffs to coals

I bend back hanging on
I hang on
Do you hang on too as I do
Whichever state swivels up next

I return a little past the starting point
I change rooms
Changing blooms, I tend to face sun
Except on bad days with rugs rolled

I'm like the Great Wall of China
I'm like the oceans too
All of the above like I am
Screen out any natural likeness

I go off the deep end and come up in shallows
I I I all I think about, I
Is that any way to fun anyway
Tibet it is

FOR LAFFS

as you read this you should learn
to do something

if not about yourself, at least your neighbor
perhaps something disturbing will please
so you overactivate a gland

as far as to yourself
leave *that* to your neighbor
allowing to him (or her)
the pleasures of retaliation
and you the pleasure of imagining
relationship buds

when you're all through
another day will have passed
letting you sleep soundly
as night borders your bed of events

STRAIGHT ON BEARING LEFT

skies skid into Baghdad
out of my mind   copied, pieced
together, studied and translated
they get their oil from a 'well'
as likable as chinese writing systems
I grasp and share, like a popping beacon,
the *complete* experience of the sky's members
whose i.d. cards are clouds
(see conditions inside) and how they bend

A lulls B into seeing D
R loves S but hates you
Z snores as Y marks the spot with X
ledge ages dawdle, and rush,
as I pull plug out, and rug E

STANDARD AIR

Craziness
Of sun on Sunday
Flocking to fair
Thru dirty air
Wind cells
Weep till x
Crosses with r
Leading to h
We hex babies
Sovereign
Pulsations submerging
Tacks along the border
In w's with pink
Sails   None back
Down toward the South
Central States playing
Tag along with
A bunch of relaxed rivers
Terrific pressure
Moves down from temples
Where assuring folks
Kneel alongside
Our body
Cutting out z
Lateral motion
Floating
Thru heat tremors
Wiles ache away colors
Sideways while
Mr and Mrs Sideways
Salaam
Whirring longevity

The buzz
Alaska shook east
Ages a horizontal coast
A yellow t-coast
Whisks surf into
An orange, filtering
Out the coats our
Movie senses land in
Heat
Of the water
Rose
Partial carmine
Imprinting stupendousness
Supporting pants
With quarrelsomeness
Habits street clouds star
We huff and
Puff
Pervious to purviews
Echoes having us floored
Give us an i
I
Give us an m
M
Gulp we got
Statements of poll
Utants milling
About the national brain
Back inside, among
The cards
The sense creeps
We never left
Around n and o
Everyone corr

Oborating
Our fleet
Prayed
Atmospherics

PRIME MEAT CLOUDS

prime meat clouds
personality (weird mood changes) dependent
on weather (see handwriting about)
sun shines, makes no diff   it's all one
whatyamacallits extend into a twilight futurity
lightly lumped   whozits forgets (I guess)
what kind of shit was for lunch
yesterday   all that's known (visible)'s
whozit's whatsit   a green (leaves) and blue (sky)
fracas embroils the horizon (horizontal) like a livingroom
and whatsisface, with broom, sweeps clean
thingies and thigamajigs on wobble into and out of consciousness
like exhausted huffing cunts   the vertical is
puffs   illustrations are in fantasy dust
grassy and gesturing and down to earth
one woman
one man
one moment

LOOKS LIKE A BUSY WEEK

fog over the city this day
brings neither-here-nor-there coolness
through the window to my left
traffic is morning-like but quiet
getting used to and keeping
the week back in the weekend
afternoon and evening've already started
to take shape place in my mind
this afternoon read this evening type

TO USE

like
a
drop
of
water
risen
from
the
sea

HAPPY / DOLPHIN

happy
dolphin

looking back

send
work

COME IN AND LOOK

energy F,A,C,E
rests in the pocket of a collar
the wind whistles at an oil truck humming
Z memory
plays with some dowels
and builds
around
right now
away
a lounge in the early morning
a swing through the H's puts the lights on the I
F drops an ace
as fresh (drop) as a rose the ace of hearts
hello, ace
zzzzzzzzzz
(no answer)
hello, hearts
zzz (thump) zzz (thump) zzz (thumzp)

THINKING

left hand under left ear
elbow leaning
body relaxed
right eye staring to the right
about: something
about nothing in particular
left eye half-closed

interior synthesis breakfasts on
insides ABCDEFG, F bumping E and G
outside, U, grown beyond recognition
waits while CB and D and A embroil
lots of distance $2^{1/2}$ inches, one cubit
is covered   my elbows rest
hands massage my temples (prayer-time)
C and D pitch and roll
a thought like a 10 lb. sack of sugar at rest on
palms begins to weigh me down
it is an L-shaped thought brocaded with
hearts all over,   O, V, E
replenish in the plain of R's
it fleets soon to the beyond (B rattles F)
down the block
the wind gets dense
the beyond reverberates
the room Y's and unwinds O, N
my ears are earrings to her the's
she sleeps and wakes my days

THIS IS THE RIGHT

This is the right
Time and place
To put on the right face
This is the right hand
Clutching zinnias in the spine
This is the right side of the brain
Where a flower bed
Entices the right person to sleep
This is the right turn
We're supposed to make not miss
To get to the party
Right there this party is
To the right of the light house
Right in the garden

THE PEARS ARE THE PEARS

the pears are the pears
the table is the table
the house is the house
the windows are the windows

the car is the car
the roads are the roads
the streets are the streets
the white line is the white line

the curves are the curves
the thigh is the thigh
the knee is the knee
the arms are the arms

the eyes are the eyes
the mouth is the mouth

SWAN LEG

the central vision
's in the oven
with the chicken
the dishes are
in the sink
the kitchen
's in the livingroom
with the heat
in the radiator
the person is
on the couch
absorbing the heat
the vestibule
's in the hall

THE WORDS TO THE SONG

the words to the song were about
love   and love is about
life   life, life is about
art while art is about
everything

the american word for everything is "art"

so, when we talk about
everything we're really talking about "art"
did you bring everything
everything was ready
love doesn't mean *everything*

everything is about to draw to a close
but first, a song about love life and art

AH !

for Susan Hall

the pink room
the pink bed
the pink sheet, covers
and spread on the bed
covered with a pink canopy
the pink wastebasket and desk
the pink carpet
the pink phone waiting for dates
the pink bear and dog resting on
the pink bulge on the bed
the pink books
on the pink bookshelves
the pink dresses hung neatly on
pink wrapped hangers in the pink closet
with pink sliding doors
the pink dresser drawer
the pink sweaters blouses panties
stacked neatly between pink socks in pink piles
among a couple of pink body stockings
the pink tiled bathroom
smelling nice pink carpeted
next to the pink windows with pink
venetian blinds opened a slit to let in a pink sun
through pink curtains
the pink body lying among the room
flesh pink and washed and brushed
scrubbed like love with pink blond down
the pink legs and feet
pointing to the pink chandelier on the ceiling
lit by pink bulbs
pendants illuminating pink thighs

pink thighs
illuminating pink lips
with pink down
and lips illuminating the interior pinkness
aimed like a pink slipper
into the pink sky
tiptoeing briefly on the pink clouds
outside the pink room
bearing pink down
with a pink bow
like a pink heart getting pinker
and pinker pinker

OTHER VASE

blue stalls in the white
sky wind
like flowers
toss the last of the stems
illuminated towers, white
hot burn
the eye through the roof
trouble getting started
trembles in the presence
of trouble finishing
high gloss
getting higher under chamois
sticks with one pain
I look through and through
nothing reminds me of you
the turns get no further
touched with lavender

RESTLESS

scanning the outer world
with my senses the inner world
bumps against a tree in a park
filled with strollers after rain after hot morning
with a large dog pissing against the bark
a wind so it seems
hot from all the activity
is arriving in a car circling the block's blood
for the millionth time (it happens so fast)
looking to park and does across from a store
crowded with shoppers entering and leaving
the revolving door revolving charges
plates and kids clutched in the hand in the pocket in the bag
my ear (left) is bumping into a radio
that moves rapidly past in the hand of a stroller
while the other ear barges through two couples
dressed up and looking down the street discussing where to eat
my feet ache from a long walk in the rain and are wet
sogging my legs as my heart coughs through its hangover
a little faster than the cigaret I puff
windows
windows
street-crossers
sidewalk movers-over
a slowing down, all,
to catch up with the hotter parts of nerves
a seamless fatigue
tailored to the city like a flush
a seeing of brain upon the gates
doors and windows open and close to exits and entrances
light travels
shade cools

sound carries
animal vegetable mineral
here and there are heroes and villains

HUMAN EVENTS

I
picked up
a shovel

and started
digging

pretty soon
I was
in china

and started
walking

ALWAYS/SURPRISED

always
surprised
people
think
about me
and
recommend
me
to
their friends

POEM

the gun raised and fired at the man next to
the blue car   the man washed his car, dusted the
dashboard, cleaned out the ashtrays, hosed the
mats, and put a terrific shine on the hood as the
bullet was traveling his way   when the bullet got
there all was left was a few bars of music coming
out the window of the shiny car going around the
bend   the bullet succumbing to the charms of night
and fog lazed around on an imaginary elbow day-
dreaming   as the music died — night was falling
at the time — the bullet decided to return to bed
and dream in the assassin's gun   when the bullet
got to where the barrel had been the barrel and
the assassin were gone, too   so the bullet just
fell down where it was, snoring under a bush
dreaming of night and fog stranded with a date

SHE LOOKED

she looked at him

and got up

without saying a word

an hour later

SATURDAY NIGHT

Martha wears a mu-mu
and Ellen has a boo-boo
Bill has a beautiful b-b
and Morris has everything

Turk has a cigaret
and Michael has Ellen
Zeke has a bandanna
and Martha loves it

Louise has a thought
and Martha's in it
Zeke has Louise handy
and Bill plays blues

Martha Ellen Bill Morris Turk
Zeke Michael and Louise

GOES ON

The beat
Comes out the speaker
Bodies start to move
Yearning to be
Next to leaning
On some other body
They get up to dance
Couples a common
Denominator although
A few threes and fours
Can be seen
Around the floor
Spines showing through
Clothes take on
Unearthly glow
As if all things
Unthought of when
In the course of events
Have surfaced
Having a good time
Between songs
Everyone stands around
Breathing saying
To each other
What fun
Is the next one fast or slow
Can I have this dance
Who wants to know

FOR JOAN

2 things
come to mind when I
think of you   perfume and
sunspots   not the same
2 things that came
to mind a little while
ago on the porch
legs and ass   the day
doesn't mind me spinning
my brain into
a rug of afternoon
under the feet
you are many things for a person
and many people for one person

BODY

the people in it
they are gray babbling
pressed forward (toward B)
by fingers of hands
settling down (in a delta)
like a river
green-blue and brown
along the nerves of the fields
an eye (of A)
follows the original sensations
like a school of fish
learning (something, B) to the unknown
according to the people in it according
to the green branches talking to the people in it (ah!)

ONE FOOT

one foot in the other world
the other foot in the other world

THE PIANO SHIVERS

the piano shivers
someone's singing through
the radio through
shrugged shoulders
his tongue rolling over black keys
each note like a bone
added one by one to a skeleton
the sky, flesh, brings
the beast back to life
it walks upright
snacking on hedges
low-hanging twigs
low flying planes
the song lands at three points

GETTING THROUGH

for Alison

when you been somewhere else
the balls turn on their feet and head away
to a horizon or moment that clangs

too often a decision is made a discussion
and sprouts like weeds lots
with paths hidden in the growth
to be followed by feet

and often a sigh
can be seen with its fingers
strangling the daylights out of the day
turning white in a rose sunset

a chant is heard for dawn   :
O dawn, get your ass here quick
do not keep the livers and diers in suspense
they await your breakfast image

those that have been at prayers
of one thing or another all the night

sleep

work

play

the generals of meditation align
in little sacks of notions to be worn
like flapping ties on the neck in the wind

O little steps to services
and the changing economy of insanity
brood on the still waters of the soul
the next brood flushes with a whoosh

could be a balance
in the grand movement
of universal semblance
adapted by the goers and comers

the horizon dips
and dips
the left and right hemispheres
that organize the fears

with oceans are still little ears

GERM WARFARE

Windows slam open under A, for aggression,
While O, for open, languishes under A, for anguish
Under U, for utter, more windows and a little v, for vines,
Next to B, for brow, I love you,
For under N limps Q

When last seen, under deranged, W for windows
Banged into a K-like coast
Packed to the nines with boats and boats
Carefully seething

Stress, for instance, joined by a wrist and a heart
Lazed in the sea touched by a rumpled O

STRANGE / DREAMS

strange

dreams

splash

water

on

the

face

boil

water

for

coffee

make

music

on

the

radio

BLAZING DOWN SUN

blazing down sun
through glow through window
warn of spring, body
expanding all pores
out to the day that jettisons
its yellow cups
fine fingers with tiny
sources of light move
across the river movement
of the body making
the organism bulb
the mental room light
and airy to stretch out in
saying "look inside, see how"
and after a second a smile
a clearing
a clearing of the throat
a song of wonder and surprise
perch on a fence

BLINK

for Manfred Hecht

the management
organized
the company
and that was splendid
enough chairs for all
a quick change
of clothes and scene
brings us
to
the
lawn
of the company
stretching out under our gaze
which itself
beer in hand
stops short of the horizon
(grazes)
everything
else
vanished
a certain rhythm (uncertain)
of the blood
directed
attention
to the tapping foot
was this happiness being witnessed
was this many weeks
did the people over there
look same as the people
over there (hmm)   who were
they

were
they
salesmen   could we brush
aside the tapping
that by now had given way
to winking
and that to sleeping
and then to tapping again
what was being
what was being covered up   was it
a fabulous shoulder
gleaming   was it an
exact (and exacting) self-image
suffering no
monkey business   were they
happy   did the countryside
bloom, did not subside
who were they   were they
salesmen   and given
fresh air
and sun   who
were their wives   were
they salesmen, too from here
they look
organized and
like good company
not
to overlook
the flowers and facts
what were they doing here   had
they
been invited   did
they receive
invitations   with what grace

was it many weeks   they "you
bet I am" emotion
reflected (a shoulder)   whose
were they
sales
men (and women)
did they make rounds   and (ooph)
how spiffy did
they look   did they look up
as the management
passed
threading toward the logo-decorated dais
were they
former salesmen (and women)   did
they look it   what was
their
country
of origin   was it organized   who
did they think they were   (or weren't)
how did they look
in the light of the
flowers of the facts
were they news   the kidding aside
the beer flowed
the lawn rolled endlessly
in and out like a boat
a picture of waves   was
a storm brewing   when
vacations
came around were they still
to be
salesmen (and women)   and retirement
what
about

retirement
but who could be retiring
under
the gentle hand of
unlimited beer and lawn
were those beer-colored
storm clouds rolling in
were
they
invited   were
they salesmen (and women)   where
did they come from   would
they go
away
could they be covered
up   why were they unresponsive
to good sense   and why
were they gleaming
did this look like
a
good
place for rain
to retire in
would rain fall
without
invitation   would it spoil
the company
what effect would it have
on
self-image
would the people
look
the
same

after the rain   were they
salesmen (and women)   why
were they gleaming   did
the self-image include shoulders
were they inviting
were they cloud-like
were they salesmen (and women)
organized
to manage a quick change
was the self-image
good company
was
it
a salesman or a saleswoman
invited to
be
a manager
would they make the dais
what about the clouds
were there
enough
chairs
for all the managers
would they live
happy
in those chairs after
they were
managers   would they
settle for chairs

SUPERFLUITY

breathing easy, "mulch", again, again things fall as
river rubs eyefolds
rainfall into place again, watching

a green hedge creep into a slate cloud, watch-
". . .feel?" ing a hedge creep into hedge,
watch a cloud creep into hedge,
watching hedge turn cloud
and, wrapping into a light spray,
out of reach
turn cloud hedge, and, coupling

eye and eye, right, rest easy
". . . . ." what —
boring : ring ; boring into border ; chip
wing falls,
away — say you say,
ice pitons, lemon, climb folds,
suns in face, touching raining

WASH

Ruga pith running high
Sleeping mat past early dawn
Thru involved vessels
In a white hat —
In high tension, and red nostrils
Blending into the white wall
Cutting a widestreak clear
Wash, ruddy, and candy samples
Out of the white sky,
Night gravel under the tree
And lighting the new sand
Mountain, rising terrible
As I kneel into drinking water.
Golden.   Behind bare oak.
Naptharunning wind over the bay

BACKSCRATCH

such
is a fluke

dashes
across the bottom
of the water

very deep
and
very blue
and
very watery

from here

I stand

fishing
for weather
balloons

outside
my shirt

very
first thing
in the morning

COOL/COOL

cool
cool
air
dips
into
an
artery
just
as
fingers
tip
the
water

CANDLING

is thread
of something that leads in
to the heart

gold

midas touch of
sense turning sense
senseless

and, making a mocking
bird of
eyes and hands

a fire in
the wind

is a thread
of
molding blood molding

slipping sandily
thru my fingers
a yolk

of fabric fracturing
my shell

shell crumb
ling without show
wing a crack
as skull crumbles
touching whole

world and turning
it shell

is a thread thread
ing its way

leading in plumbing
low melting
point of my inner
shell
rising at
shadowdrop or windgust
and,
soars over trees

my skull with
out a tail with
out dressing
sours phosphorescently
to its name

is a thread
un
raveling
revealing
reveling

forming
rope then cable

and, watches me
consuming a still
life, hard

boiled egg with
out wine, and, bread, or salt

cut by light
stream pouring gild on
table

and, that light
lets
and, lets
other half
wait til

I make sense
of having
of
line between cut, and, shadow

taut

relieving blood in leech
is hatching
there
is

FOOD CYCLE

clean glass
dark park and buildings
part night
lights clear
and then I look in
to find my weariness
I wear my work and its dust
over my body
passing into a wonderful darkness
on the other side
morning wakes
it is not late   it is *just* right
I wash and shave
smoke a cigaret
have some coffee
my body wakes up
that was a long time ago
my body wakes up
tired
frazzled
snow
snow turning to rain

SUCH A LONG TIME

such a long time
such longing
brings us to this place
in the plural
such destruction of the soul
such wanton soup
flying up to devour sunset
and pour down
through holes in sky's throat
to remind us where we are
such delicacy
like a spiffy hook
in place of a delicate hand
gracefully doing what fingers do
reaching across the table
reaches the fast food
a fast logic sets in
and we set it off
with such a wonderful
few words you could
hardly believe those were
your own charms
such they impressed
a slope of back
a slope of hill
such is the state of
elements, and their statement
much todo
much to do

HAND OVER

0

woozy
if
window
the
wealth
if-windows
of
notions (?)
potions
power-hungry
cigaret
less
treat
theater
to another one
(I've a notion to
elbow
way
up
stargaze
wet
hands
dryer

1

give
you
(a quick
less hungry

look
to
ward
toward
that ether
sprit
(out sidemouth
sidesaddle
notion
of
hyphen

0

from what I
under
fluid
lance
of
stand there
(no.   there...(?)
stand
route
forehand
clone
tread
bag
gauge
stream out I
ear
closer to (and)
notional
dispersal

1

develop
pills
(to quicken
hards
out
of to a
first idea
stand
that
let
(honk
that
let
bonked on a
head
move on
(stand
ahead
stand
on a
(stand
head
loop
in us
term
in us (to(?)
pedestal

0

well
that

(to thicken
the ater
up
(get off the
ground
does

1

the
after
(astir
dips down quick
in an (I)
flash
hollers
(to...
all fours
rushes
claps

GHOST

feeling enters
listening to the frag
watching me walk
to the fire, walk to the fire
to confirm whether "I sit here boring"
feeling withers
in flame or is hint
ing mint and salt
"directly...huhn?...said and done"
just so much cold

steam
that's moot
hind cat's feet are moot
that is, they match each other preter
morph having the ties that bond
leaving damp paisley prints be
gat on white kentile
that's, if cat moves
hind around a lot, para
mecium fashion be

"see that
my hat fell off
it's raining gray
felt hats here by the sea"
gat getting back to fee
kissed me like I was never kissed be
fore feeling soot falling on back
of my hand with
out feeling gritty to tears
almost cried a pinch of salt

"my heart in my mouth"
rants without getting rancid about the whole thing
or, nasty colors, clogged, for that matter be
gat, and, in my throat rushing to the sink
with the same breath, then kissed me
to plunge hand in
washing white mottle girding fur
grit down drain when
I pull out the rustcracked plug

I hear voice spinning
words clockwise when
at me your
when underhand moving
thighs counterclock
wise straws in my bel
ly be
gat
shouldn't, and, I shouldn't
feel loose about a sud
den hind rap in the stomach

                          (in distance : rivetgun gat
                          (linga preter rivets into I
                          (beams naturally be
hind gat breaking thru lath and plas
tern unfinished picture of your hanging
hand which is desiccatingly fine in front, lying
rust and plum
from reaching plasma and paintsheen
a cloud on fog feet
if one two or etc removed looks
at it without leaving a mark

                                    turn board look tick
ling a memory bottled from the right angle
across my mat frameback tingly pre
venting light etch from rip
pling mater
ially thru cracks be
meant tick getting settling

NEXT WEEK

for Ed. Baynard

the man sat crosslegged on the bench
in the rain (which it's doing out)
uttering thoughts
"poetry is verifiable by looking
out the window   or for that
matter looking in"
and he (the man) did for awhile

he passed through infinite being skirting eternal life

he took hold by the toe of infinite power and sailed through boundless
    space

he intoned universal law and read by the candle of omnipresent light

he felt the waves of omnipotent consciousness get born grow up go away
    and die

and swelled with all-embracing love

to the cosmic rhythm that whirled and flashed like winds around his
    body

he fell free from the grip of ever-present creativeness

and landed in the lap of unlimited knowledge

thus it happened that, the rain fell
and the man sat
putting a roof on the house of his body
every once in awhile he uttered a thought or two
but most of the time
he was a window for others to look through

clean glass
bright branches
wind (wind)
springlike sun
and wind
crisp (edges)
inking
again brilliance
the feeling to lie low
a blue overcoat
six instruments
a melody, who with
sawdust
a broken pipe
can you drive
a glass of beer
telephones
we wait
an air of thinking
street
half-months
bathwater
eau-de-cologne
ages ago

sit down, clean glass
your name is in the paper
your car from which water drips
is thinking about you longing
for the longest time
confidentially leaning across offices afternoons
getting some fresh air in your trunk
will you call any evening
like a skylight through some vowels
or will you puff gently along the outer ear
are you laughing recently
at the pleasure machine and fun knocking
too good to be true your sitting here
and too sure felt, but don't take off
your story is of an elephant lady
hunched over a detailed jungle
singing a song

clean glass
and sky
pink light blue
building lights
a laugh (ground floor)
direction, anything new
thoughts to night
leaves and branches
in the way
in the way you walk
in the cleaning and cooking
in the clear
a sigh of relief
rubs against feet
on the first floor
melancholy

O, clean glass
this is the morning
the year rolls onto its end
scrawny with handwriting
faces
make faces
look that face up in a soap book
believe it or not
we are witnesses of an endless chair
rattling around
very long from now
we will look back at all this
through our papers
noticing exactly where like a swan
attention pays to drift

clean glass
christmas fire
crisp my heart
this song
whole earth
people around
they play
at life
they don't mind
the same thing
next day
snow out
heart out
breath out
the piano plays
carry my love out
garbage

clean glass
a pond light
wolf bay
work spread out
shows himself
face too heavy
like an index
as I see a sheet of music
a communal roar
24 hrs
a normal social life
may die
may die
flamingoes of curiosity
feet on the cliff
young notes seem
are these our parents
are these our children
a surface of light blue trees

here I am, clean glass
breathing easily
even in anxiety
the winds of winter chill my pains
for yours
sliding between me
and the world (and the world)

no rest to bother about

photos, she would say
is that her awash in the park
snow play anymore

anyway
I wanted to say
how I feel
with a peculiar accent
knowing you would understand
don't you
look, your brown hair and powder blue sky

clean glass
car horns
the look the look
between
the paws
the sound of crumbled notes
home
moment
float
alcohol
hint of clouds
same language spoken
memory listens
that's what I said, yes
uh-ha

clean glass'
other year
the players nod hello
little stories
tea with milk this
first morning where
the tramping elephants
are muffled by snows that
have fallen are falling have
fallen   wait up, flakes
remember day flakes
green with vegetable minutes
someday unlike today which
is wishful thinking
what are you thinking of
what are you thinking   where is
the elephants' graveyard
O clouds if only for a minute
before the tape is ripped from
your foreheads try and enjoy

clean glass
well seated on a go-stone
wake with a start
is all is well
the grass parts as it has come
heralding bamboo and water guns
hiss   (slipping down)
writing (at center) around one hand
four directions across a room
silence guards
a pond or river with a natural sound
imitates a long day
it is today
in a particular shape
in the shape of a trumpeting heart
on the chest
great distance leak through

on without them
furled along the outermost cool slopes
under the droop baby-lip become
the clean glass
roll up like a shade
snap out of it   I have been...
who cares
deluxe medium point
distraction, O tires

clean glass
lone thread that follows itself
wind up cupped
one-on-one it is clear   woo-woo's
an improvement smokes in arms
a tale of china sit upon the plate
a grove in florida the movies
crissed and crossed
recall living in a house in an ear nursery
brooding
infection
invention
grab trouble
O, prairie
aunts and uncles to fall guys
weave the spirit heard in the first talkie

HOWDAH

there's something I want to know
shawled
music
hello, you
me too
glancing at a whole world of figures
full of the back seat
the speaker filled (music) with pauses
studying the nature (shawled) of inference (launched)
some sort
uh . . . . . well . . . . .
widely (shawled)
guess I do
hello, you
me too
personally isolations other shoe
interacts with the ear and the floor
slowed to a crawl very rapid (me too)
dimension (eyes closed) snags
more bangs
acting up (shawled)
take a what
(music) about to run

then let's go O then
indoors turn a blue
anybody or not
cheerfulness or joy
about others (music)
love (shawled)
voice weathered
where's your girl (hello, you)
me, too

THE MUTT'S LASER

green packages are on the trees
the wall is filled with green parcels
the sky's so blue the green consumes me
light and shadow
stumble through the breeze around my arms
resting on elbows on table, airfoils
take off

the yellow towel
the yellow towel with the darker yellow flowers on it
make the rack a hanging yellow garden
in the green room
with the tile sky
a plane flies over everything
is a helicopter
is a sound of a helicopter
is going now

a leg aches under the yellow green blue and red afghan
on the blue blanket
on the white sheet
on the green and white sheet
as everything is matchless

it would be real easy
to change this work around
and mosey elsewhere
which impulse I'll put down
to laziness and easiness

but I can talk about
the causes for all this mild affection

forming a puddle in my heart
when learned "ought" says flood
"ought" stays down

the head with the brown hair
needs a wash
is attached to the neck
needs a wash
is pinned to the shoulders
have a hunch
leaning over the chest
over the desk
and the rest of the body
from waist to toe sits in a lap
and everything needs a wash
is too lazy to get up and get one

a voice somewhere says
under the buzz of a small plane
"hey, sweetheart   you need a jacket?"
and a window opens
under the tweet of a clothesline
under the chirps of birds

dog bark
dog bark
the golden afghan in the backyard
sleeps like a little lion lying
across the path
from door to door
more tweets

the green is moving
in time to the breeze

attaches imports to the demands
exporting themselves from the tongue
exhales moving feelings in
skybound wheeling
better for the moment keep excess down
and there make a little farm
some country in the city
some "hey!" in afternoon's barn

THE LIFE

for Joan

a boring moment
I pick up a book of poems written by boring poets
the poems aren't good they aren't bad

they get jobs
they get wives and children raise families
they write poems
they live interesting lives

I'm getting pissed off
pissed off
I pick up a pen and start to write
I take a break
burn most of my old poems
throw out letters
dump boxes of papers
I get back to work
there are poems and *poems*

there are limits to what I can put up with
there are those make me want to puke over my shoulder

night steals into afternoon
and mugs one
formal like a dress, the coming of winter
what trees there are
lose leaves and gain edge
while I get my winter nerves
something weird's going on in my left shoulder
like a crazy parakeet
banging against bars of muscles and bone
whims drive cars into the garage of the blood

there are rush-hours and images of sadness
making the nose flute
there are beer senses searching for a rug to be snug in
the hand turns to winter
and raises a landscape to the nose
and the nose knows

a man was sitting
on a crag poring
over a book   he looked
through the picture window
of his soul and said
"it's rainy   it looks like
rain   I wonder if it'll rain"
his skin grew damper
through the evening
and the pages turned
themselves after awhile
the corners of the room
beat into night
like eagle wings
the man looked out again
a curtain was drawn
by an interior pair of hands
turning instantly to a window
the man went
to California to have a look
returned for season changes
in the meantime
finished the book

you *are* a poet

your feet are long fellows
and the yellow stars
hang in a jar

dredging up the edgy motion of conversation
jump on dawn's hat as slime meanders to the drain
nerves drain into the bed
with a passle of muscle
and construct
canals and bridges to invade dreamland

so *what's* new

the lecturing side of the moon
tonight rests in an earring
on the lobe of the person
listening to the stirrings of *your* person
and whispers passion like a half a pear
to the dish between us
mist decorates with a couple of spoons
and clanks distract

wrap some words in a coat
and send them out in the night to you
and hope they catch on on your street
embrace your window with thuds and rattles
kicking you into your slippers and robe
before your think neighbors'll come to probe

come to me
the words will say
and you will
and only I'll know
what hit you

a slice of paper
slices into your life of water
splashes out of the glowing pool
and becomes a part of my life
making my face shine
a
smile
discovered to be around the globe
joins us like a belt of forces
holding the world, sea for buckle
the mood holds to the refreshment stand
where we stand have lunch hold hands
hear our clothes

from the belly
a thin web
starts to shine
the sun
starts to climb
each strand
until it reaches
in my gray matter
and burns
it red
and sets with
delight and starts
another day with
light after light

a woman sat in a room getting larger and smaller
as
each
day
passed

looking in and out like a fuck
to the moment
when the earth would begin to shake
and rock in time

one day her ass was too big
and she felt uncomfortable
one day her tits were too small
and she felt uncomfortable

the room began to disturb her sleep
as well as her waking
as she longed for some sort of satisfaction
it came about like a boat
that
she
sat
for
many
years

her voice
flew in the sky like a bird
her body bathed in the water created by her hand
her mind made the colors of the passing day
each day into a bath to bathe the birds who flocked to her

she was content after awhile to sit and rest

as she passed the room one day
she looked in
and
was
astounded
she said to herself "this is wonderful"

and she felt as much
and last time she heard she enjoyed keeping in touch

isn't it strange how ambition
takes on a high and bright language
almost rushing into a play with murders
as it crosses the mind like a roach crossing the wall
it's something I have
like
an
apartment
and something I admire in others even if
I feel misdirected   the energy is terrific
and soothes and rubs like a towel after someone's bathed
it's the difference between indifference
loosening furry bonds chomping on the brain
as someone, pressed, says
I've lost my train   why can't you be more realistic
and that's what I am
only I'm making everything up from scratch
and can hear even the tiniest feet
strolling along on white flat

bundling noises enter my ear
and release a catch to many synapses
something is starting to take place,
I want to tell you, don't you think you should ask
I'm running out the door
running out of things to say
"stay awhile" I thought and did
and want to say to you   "stay awhile"
does this sound like a complaint
vaulting out of the imploring hand over
the bar of the heart
ear of the cup of woes

morning dreams
afternoon dreams
evening dreams
night comes in sits down and dreams
the ashtray dreams the cigaret its smoke
the hand bracing my head dreams of writing down dreams
upstream, a dream starts to take root in the river
as a sliver of light dreams a shiver in my spine
the back waves bye-bye to the brain
a hand writing the dreamy words
"this is them"

smooth and bumpy wonder meet in a tongue
licks the lip of the day
something special (instantly forgotten) brings this on
forms a landscape
adds a little motion makes a scene

for some odd reason
when a poem comes to mind these days
the opening line always includes
the words "strange" or "weird"
as
the strange sense
the weird voice
and this puzzles me
does this come from some strange boredom
flowering in a garden both mental and actual
making me feel weird
"flowers" or "flower" like some platonic likening
take root and put in their appearance
in the actual
                    in the actual what
that's something entirely different

as the chest lowering into the belly is
and why not
it's *that* (hold two fingers barely a-
part) close
someone's making a lot of noise chewing
and that takes on a weird importance
as if this poem
is a meditation on distraction
a voice lighting in the breeze to someone else
some other "you"
points OUT like a finger raised in a sign
to the somewhere else where "me" is
and at that, too, "someone"
lets me know the strangeness
brief contact leaves behind like
a knife is souvenir
and useful when is open

beneath
the bulging tiles
is the wall
to find it
you have to pick up
yellow and blue towels
hanging on the rack
and imagine your way through
the white speckles
if more realistic
take finger
and push in tile
after the initial surprise when
bulge disappears to
floor
you'll notice there's the wall
yes, there's the wall

today everything is beautiful
tomorrow, maybe so
that's not what I'm really thinking
thinking of you
thinking of you
both of you've made everything beautiful before
think you can do it again?
let me know
while everything is still pretty beautiful

a lug drops into the hubcap
on the wheel of life
I'm wearing for hat today
with an entrance and exit painted "feminine"
and the color of the sky "aspirin"
the way a tablet starts
to dissolve on tastebuds at back of the tongue
running out of spit at the curved moment

knocking's driving me and the city crazy
and as the streets start to wobble
a haze starts to crumble into bits of blue
and a moon-disk, the sun, is visible
as the wheel is audible
as the wheel is manageable

the knee's the window
to
the
leg   the leg
of the house   and
the door   that's the brain's
knob   the knob
turns through history

like a swan turning on
the water   inspiration
the faucet in beak
wants
to
speak
to
the
spoon   the ankle spoon
slurps in full-view
day's feet

the thought of the girl
reached back into time and space
the tongue of the universe
and her tongue were one
stars fell around her
and lighted on her clothes
as her legs went into a million positions
the position of the rose
the position of the peony
the position of the iris, of the tulip
her eyes were rainbows
and her eyebrows bows from which sprang glances
her ass applause
her heart a sauce in which
the thought was smoothed
over which she guided
a gold tooth

we carried our rug with us
everywhere   we'd come to a village
and put the carpet down
the people threw us petals or glances, depending

we slept on it
ate on it
lived on it   when it was time to go home
we cut it into bits
and each person took part
my part has birds and clouds
and a tear of bordering grasslands
I keep it near the window
tend it carefully
water it
clean it with a fine spray of air
and carry it with me
whenever I'm away from home
I have it with me today
you may step on it if you wish

beauty but lent
like an apartment
asks that pleasure
pay the rent

as quote coats
words in the throat
let my tongue
bend like a bell
each consonant

and let me send you
a package of vowels
and with them
a terrific view

love returns what you sent

better step on it
got to get there fast
wherever there is
and get there
without messing clothes
working up a sweat
striking a pose
relief!   dazzling
belief fuses my body
with the landscape body
white smoke surrounded
by the aura of red fire
fades in the sunset wire
step on the sunset wire

at least a thousand alphabets
clog the universal throat
wheels turn in the larynx
brings about a swell
brings the neck low
next to the fiery breath of the earth
a letter sealed in an envelope
like a white chair jumps in the sky
sliced like pie
on other hand Lizzie's
standing on her head, shaped like a hand,
with a banana sitting on the ground
she is in the throat
and so is the tutu around the words
dancing out of habit in the discovered streets
sheer logs like stockings
moving over the river
move over the liver
then there's the spleen

"hey, Lizzie   you seen my spleen?"
she doesn't answer

a necklace of cities
tagged with shadows
from the plane
a sandbar extends like a ruff
around the watery neck
dreaming of a speck

we move in the distance
like dancing foothills
complementing horizontal trees
walk on top of the brush

lopsided night subsides
as we decide to unload
the last of the bundles
we carry as we made them

the long diagonal fan of water
moves swiftly from the plug
dancing cars
bare feet and cool brows
instant like forms
echo in sublime dorms
the street moves through glistening
and races to the sewer
various cool things
hang on the grate like categories
you speak about "paper cups"
I listen to "dogshit"

the body
rattles bones

in agreement
nods its head
with various personalities
in an all-day glass
the arm sips the
knee slips keeps
moving in the house

a plaza
whirls into place
under
the
shoulders
where the building
's more sky than window
art sits next to a pigeon
waving "arms"
I'm affected by the scene
rushing into my feet
I
decide
to
do
something
about it
circle the block
circle the idea of the block
a beautiful woman comes
out
of
the
block
the line between us
its own plaza
I rest next to the fountains

bathing triggers
let loose fingers
from the edges of the view
everything comes together
4 years from now
with the emergence of color and pictures
both're flying above now
waiting that moment
when the mind has moved on
and the papers sit nifty in their twine
not too long afterward
a noise emanates from a reed
someone sits up nights
listening to the wind and his knees

the smell of hay
comes in the door to stay
in the country today
tomorrow I will be on my way
to New York and another day

the wind takes
toilet paper
off the roll and flings
it to the sky
past underwear
past shirts
past all
and slides
sheets along stratosphere
where air's thin
and the days long
and earth spins

a scent
of fall comes in
the window with the wind
every 4th breath
this heat
can't last much longer
because I can't
my mind turns easily
to a spot in time
where physical comfort
doesn't have
the upper hand
mornings are
a vase
with a flower variety
air rings   I answer
"a flower for you"
"what!   that mongrel!"
the flower bites

water
drains slowly
in
the water
the sky
reflected in
the water
moves
the green of
the water
along the
blue of
the sky

today borrows
a pinch of fall
a teaspoon of spring
to make afternoon
delicious   well, not
delicious, tasty
I borrow
a sentence here
a couple words there
to make this poem
terrific   well, not
terrific, okay
dear person, excuse
me for wasting your time
this is a little boring, no?

the sun shines
on one glass
then another
across the whole front
of the building
setting the colors
(brown green and orange)
in window frames
then traffic like
a hand on fingertips
moving west
begins to erase
everything even
through beautiful roses

one of those days
when night comes
you think you haven't

done enough   and sleep
makes you sleepy
tomorrow afternoon
when you really want to
be awake   and the day
moves over like a lover
into evening and before you
before you know it night falls
and is falling
to your feet
inside your clothes
outside the window

incredible bullet
out to see the dawn
rise a little
make window widow
the fiery lamp
caves in the door
unhinges hinges
with a single whack
like a slack season
easing skull into
the blue   the blue
I know so well
light parts of the belly
to meet demands
of one of the brains
the blue window
soon to be fired
with blue wire

something isn't missing
and is blue

see it run around
all over town

at the same time
our friend is red
and before sleep
reaches his nose down
like a damp finger
and smells the bed

as his hands age
fingers
yellow like work-gloves
palm color and dry like palms

with white afternoon
he's so much in time
with something
he hears his brain
paint drying

O how green
he is lapping his tongue
opening a long drawer in
the dresser of boredom

his brain's red
from the bed
and soon, like nice,
he's dead and turns white
and keeps turning
like spit on a silver tooth
biting the dust named Ruth

dear body
this is a continuation
of my last communication
last time I found it
necessary to contact you
and keep you up with me
how many years
3 to 4
thinking about, in my depressed
moments, the sentence
and its state
and transporting across lines
for immoral purposes
this act of man   how
fuzz on the bow of life
performs a caption
under the picture of the simple
and the syllables
ring from the elbows
like educated patches
all pipes and wines
do you remember feeling thus
as an intimate first thought of frost
brought you uncertain pleasure
felt stroking the patch
the clear edge
seemed to surround your place
grow muggy and uncomfortable
remember when Joe said it wasn't so
in a complete statement
grow down certainly out the feet
you felt part of the place
and later higher up
a laciness of place

a continuous note
bicycling from ear to ear
like a grin lighting
I've been meaning to
speak to you for the longest time
but all my present days
are descending like heat
into their last dime
sealing over the thought of you
with weather fin

I can't help saying
you're starting to disgust me some
with your shit habits
how you easily grow
to stand anything
with protest
a tiny squeek of ache
not too loud or throb
can I hope
being like some
bitchy wife or mother
for something better
or hope you have kids
they're like you,
you'll see
I think
it's best to close
get dressed
and get along
this won't be the last
talk between us, it
isn't the first
any messages?
take care

the man
was totally absorbed
in white   he turned and wiped
his invisible brow
with poetry
the words
were invisible absorbed
in white   they turned and wiped
his invisible brain
with poetry
the man
was totally absorbed
in words   he turned white
with poetry
his invisible brow

a thought
depresses a pedal
and grows louder

                    a wing

moves against
the shoulder
and grazes it
like a cow

            a playful sun
sits on the building
on the horizon
talking on and on

weaves down the street
toward me
takes my hand

tells me its story
while I stand and listen

no, I say, can't
spare any change

in my hands
I held a book
I called that book mine
the book called itself look
and made me look
I opened
to my favorite page
then closed the covers
placed book in lap
and took a nap
and took a nap

mush easily
slow down over there
completely, like lunch, wave
to who falls through
the following flower
very bunched I think
coming on feelings
like a lump
and sit there pumping
like a heart
the mechanism's complete
like a masterpiece
and gathers strength from
the onlooker
where it came from
O, dumpling emotions

why put me over falls
in a barrel
why send me up on the sky
with a pie
why don't you get lost
in the soup
such and such a group
you know you want to form
I, I mean we, we
'd be so much the better for it
so much the worse for us

stupid graphics
were conjured out of
the clear blue sky
by a clear blue eye
and then some
they lined up on the way
in the presence of the eye
and waited like cunts
to have someone say something
say something someone
do you love me?
night was falling to its knees
a breeze started to
form a line out the door
and we follow as
far as the conversation
about walking into the door
do you love me?
say something someone
sits like manners
on the fingernail of the door
pressing onlookers

to see if they're still warm
like toast, isn't it
so much the worse for us

go on on the evening
arm in arm with others
not caring too much
whose arm
I gently stroke the arm
next to me
and bring it to life in a shake
a thick shake
something tells me I'm grasping
at straws
and camels
and needles
and backs
and needless to say
we go there to stay in the song
popped right in my mind
from nowhere

this could be
a little philosophy
got us by the neck
or by the arm
what the bump is,
I'm stumped
from now on don't bother me
until I figure everything out
when I do I let you know
you can come in
when I shout "OUT!"
then we can
paint the town

sun fork
sits on blue place mat
next to day plate
later
moon spoon
sits next to
midnight knife
minute particles of food
slip through
spaces in the mat
determining
light and dark blue
a napkin of pleasure
passes across my mouth
and I pass it to you
across from me
at the table of the ages
where you do the same
we've enjoyed
consuming our way
through seasons
now
the flame's under the coffee
and sherbert ready to cool
the holiday mouth

a wending sadness
goes through you like
a note   you're on
the road somewhere
thinking about your hair
the infinity of hair
the road goes from place
to place a rose in

your hair
as your thoughts
begin to pair
they get together
like each other well enough
become Mr and Mrs
have girls and boys
grow old and sit in chairs
watching everything
around them grow
soon they are gone
you are still
on the road
the music's starting
to make you stare
you're looking
at something very few
people have heard
about and
it pleases you
like pleasure you tap
your hair in time

half-shut eyes
bended sideways
to see if
the wonderful sky
in sip
after in-sip
tasted good
certainly it did
and the shoulder
tilted too
till a whole theory

evolved to make
a good face
better than a peony

MODERN TIMES

I may feel lousy this second
five minutes ago I felt up
all this presence brought to a head by an ah
who would've thought, ah...
would you, ah, like a cigaret, ah, eat
wouldn't you, ah, like to, ah, take off your, ah...

two ah's in the same breath a butterfly
(no kidding!)
a normal distribution curve
the body (center) at rest
all impulses and pulse very close to sine
could be meditative
could be a wonderful mesa
could be, ah, another one of, ah, sharp changes

did someone just sigh
(was that a used door)
could you lend me five bucks
(a dinner just what I need)
I walk through the park
the trees moan
I'm reminded, ah, of the moon
something else to wor, ah, ry about
wonder how long

NINTH STREET

old people
old people
large clouds, high
with expanses of high blue
palm frond huts
white buildings, blue trim
sea green tiles
everybody walks slow the same
the women have the same white sweater
the men have the same white shirt
bellies
very green grass and palms
everyone has a hunch
they're moving their life
into the shoulder of the road of life
water cool enough to refresh
thigh-deep out far
from the lighter green to the darker green
head for the green-blue
more women than men
no smiles
visions of the endless end of life
visions of holocausts (how easy it is to have)
visions whited buildings
growing whiter and pulsing
in the white pulse of the sun
visions of the beginning and end of work
visions of palms waving good-bye
and the sky reading the upward waving palms
light gray pebbled streets
highways and big hotels
big and little white curves

yellow light the same yellow as light through window shades
only no shades, blinds jalousies
cool breezes blowing through the moisture from the sea
very little talking
only talk, fervent deals and wheels
emphatic gestures into tubby waistbands
temple chants grazing my temple through speakers
as some misters and a missus pass the microphone
visions of vegetable stands
movies changing three times a week
lavender blue hair
blue gray hair
gray-green water with a middle layer of hazel-green
staring up at bridges cars trucks buses,
fisherman looking down straight in the deep
and reeling the lure in
visions of curves and angles
going every which way
keeping me awake longer than usual each night
till sleep takes me over
over the water with the deep blue lights
through memory
of the land with puffs of light green snow
laid out neatly as far as the eye can see
over the shoulder
visions arriving over the shoulder like gulls
visions sitting and waiting for the beach to empty
and the sun to enter the lost and found

THE WORDS DRONE ON

the word drone one
a sense of
a person in middle-age
half beautiful
moves down
the aisle of the room
the words make no sense
but crumble on impact
with the listener's ear
what this person
looked like young,
will look like old
dances smoothly
over the calm brainwaves
the words fill
the dry old structure
of the room
and fills in the seat
with swans
the listener
feels his ear and eye
merging in a foyer
someone greets him
it is the person before
him   he shakes hands
they walk into the other
room arm in arm
the arms are a figure of
speech   the speech
is from another time
the listener drops
the pretence of youth

from his muscles
and feels the words
drops of water
after a long hot shower
drop from hair to shoulder

QUIET DAMPNESS

Quiet dampness appears everywhere as if out of nowhere
Making the quiet pleasant and the light cool
Thoughts turn to wheels in wheels
And make the journey that's been contemplated so long
In the back of the mind where I keep what I want to make sure I
    remember
The hub of existence reflects spikes of light and spokes
The words rise like letters to the stars
Filled with frankness tenderness admiration and a reservoir of love
Deep as a wishing well with a penny hitting the top of the water
As thoughts put on the garments of flesh and wonderment

COMPLETE BALANCING WEATHER MEETS

Complete balancing weather meets
With the eye of complete off-balance brain
Tottering through verbs
Dew covers the shoe
With minute observations
Piling up in an organic unity life chair and sitter
Dog floats in with pipe slipper and paper
Sits partly over the instep of unshorn foot
Snores like a saw through the glories of news logs
The reader soon falls his head down in bliss
Or is it a sleep without dreams
In a city where the nose
Comes occasionally to a water-smelling patch of haze
On the face
Moving toward the river in a phrase

WHAT WERE HIS LAST WORDS

What were his last words
As he slipped through the sleeve
Of the curve of the finger
Looking down, straight into shoulders
Much it is to ask whether
Attention to light and detail
Seems nice in light of the suit
Grippers clutch the nice guy
Finding out
An hour and $1^{1}/_{2}$ countries later
How nice he really is
                    He's disgusting
But I like him you do too
There's something about him

YOU'RE WELCOME

don't
be
too surprised
if
I
show up
tomorrow

SITTING AROUND

Sitting around
Try to circle
In on
A specific point
I want to tell you about
You poke
The air out of the air
With your finger
Making your own point
(Emphasis)
Something's left out
I leave,
For emphasis

OFF THE HOOK

He is gone now
Taking his body with him
When all the time
I thought it was
The beauty of his mind
I loved

GRAY OUT

gray out
blue handkerchief
red checked shirt
white and light brown cigaret
red (gold) and white cigaret package
blue (silver) and clear lighter
black and white photos
blue magazine
black notebook
yellow green and orange book
red white and yellow book
green dotted magazine
blue and light blue pencil sharpener
white cup
yellow walls and door
black metal shelves
cordovan frame around simple black ink picture of supper
cellophane and glass over same
flesh hands
white baby clam nails
white book edges
green swirl sheets
light blue electric blanket
dirty windows
black 100-watt light
wood grain frame around light orange sailboat
black frame around rose, around tree
dim scenes from childhood
tinted spring memories from yesterday
gray matter

THE BOOK I TOSS

The book I toss is Boss
It bangs against the walls
And gets me working
I watch its thin green
Recede into a reed
And think the time right
To set the Boss right
We argue
Cops suddenly appear
I throw them and Boss
Out the window
And unscrew my ankles
I be my own boss
I be my own police

SEATED ON THE BACK

Seated on the back of my boat
Fanning evening into my face
My thoughts travel
Across the river
To the little town starting to light
Yesterday I was over there
Walking the streets
Saying "Hey!" to neighbors and friends
What are they doing now
Coming home from work
Kissing hello
Sitting to supper
Spending time with the old lady and kids
Watching the news
I have a hunch I'll never know
In the cabin
I've enough food for two
Some books to take my mind away
And a bed sleeping two
The moon's high enough now
To extend a toothpick of light
Across the water
For me to pick my teeth
A gurgling and humming pacifies
My lips
As I prepare for bed
Listening to fingers
Humming off the ends
Of the arms of the chair

POEMS / PILE UP

poems
pile up

soon
a gorge
rises

a river
runs
swiftly

below
soon

I step
on the
air

chat chat
and chat

LAST FIVE MINUTES

The long and the short
Of it is
I have to keep pushing
I feel myself
Pushing against the
Lead-in to beauty
And take a hunch through
With me
Into the halls
Where the everyday
Seems like eternity
There's no fooling around
About something
As serious
As it is beautiful
There's no match
For the feeling
That gets there
When I get there
And absolutely no sense
Of duration
And no telling
How everything turns out

ACKNOWLEDGMENTS

I would like to thank Curtis Faville of L Publications, who originally published *Common Sense*, and thank Suzanna Tamminen for reissuing it at the same time as *The Age of Reasons*.

The poem "Blink," originally published by Buffalo Press, is a substantially found poem appropriated and reformatted from *Think*, a biography of Thomas J. Watson.

Ted Greenwald was born in Brooklyn, raised in Queens, and has always lived in New York City. He is the author of over thirty books, including *Licorice Chronicles* (The Kulchur Foundation, 1979), *Word of Mouth* (Sun & Moon Press, 1986), *Jumping the Line* (Roof Books, 1999), *In Your Dreams* (BlazeVOX [books], 2008), *3* (Cuneiform Press, 2008), *Clearview/LIE* (United Artists, 2011), *Own Church* (Spuyten Duyvil, 2016), and *Common Sense* (L Publications, 1979; Wesleyan University Press, 2016). An online reader's companion is available at tedgreenwald .site.wesleyan.edu.